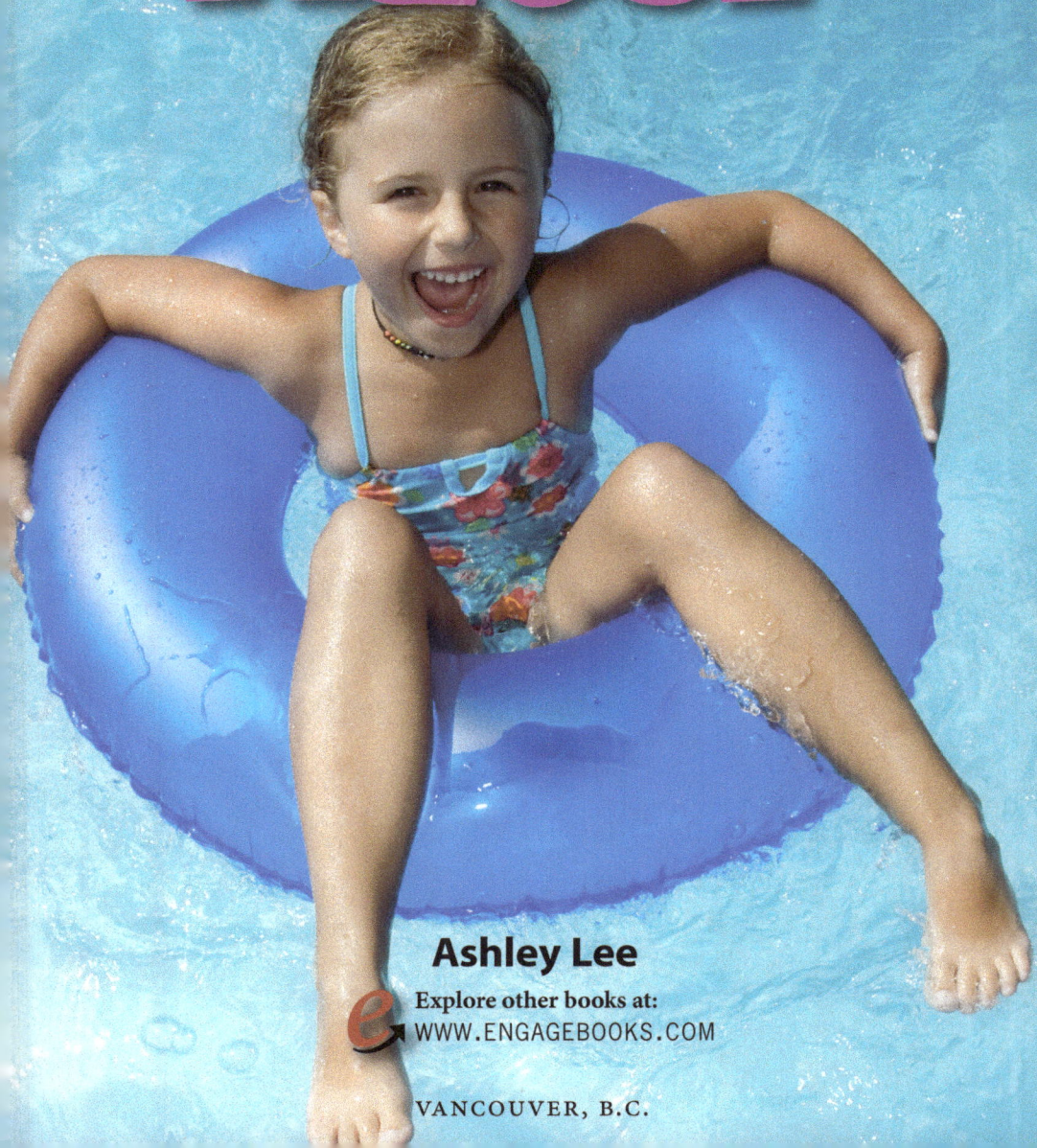

I0201565

I can HELP save EARTH

Water

Ashley Lee

Explore other books at:
WWW.ENGAGEBOOKS.COM

VANCOUVER, B.C.

e↱ WWW.ENGAGEBOOKS.COM

Water: Level 2
I Can Help Save Earth!
Lee, Ashley 1995 –
Copyright © 2021 Engage Books
Design © 2021 Engage Books

Edited by: A.R. Roumanis

Text set in Arial Regular.
Chapter headings set in Arial Black.

FIRST EDITION / FIRST PRINTING

All rights reserved. No part of this book
may be stored in a retrieval system, reproduced or
transmitted in any form or by any other means without
written permission from the publisher or a licence from
the Canadian Copyright Licensing Agency. Critics and
reviewers may quote brief passages in connection with a
review or critical article in any media.

Every reasonable effort has been made to contact the
copyright holders of all material reproduced in this book.

LIBRARY AND ARCHIVES CANADA CATALOGUING IN PUBLICATION

Title: Energy: I Can Help Save Earth Level 2
Names: Lee, Ashley, 1995- author

Identifiers: Canadiana (print) 20200309781 | Canadiana (ebook) 2020030979x
ISBN 978-1-77437-717-8 (hardcover)
ISBN 978-1-77437-718-5 (softcover)
ISBN 978-1-77437-719-2 (pdf)
ISBN 978-1-77437-720-8 (epub)
ISBN 978-1-77437-721-5 (audio)

Subjects:
LCSH: Water—Pollution—Juvenile literature
LCSH: Water—Environmental aspects—Juvenile literature
LCSH: Environmental protection—Citizen participation—Juvenile literature

Classification: LCC TD422 .L44 2020 | DDC J363.739/4—DC23

Contents

4   What is Water?

6   The Water Cycle?

8   How is Water Cleaned?

10   Water Around the World

12   Why is Water Important?

14   What is Water Pollution?

16   Water Pollution Facts

18   How Water Pollution Affects Animals

20   How Water Pollution Affects Humans

22   How Water Pollution Affects Earth

24   Water Conservation

26   Cleaning Up Water Pollution

28   The Future of Water Conservation

30   Quiz

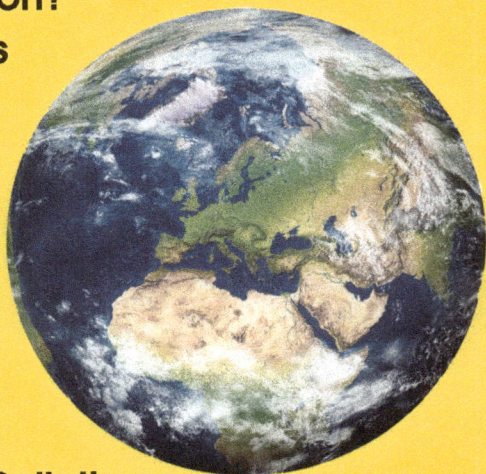

What is Water?

Water can be either a liquid, a gas, or a solid. It can change between these states when it is heated up or cooled down.

Almost seventy percent of Earth is covered in water. Only about one percent of Earth's surface water is freshwater.

KEY WORD

Freshwater: water that is not salty. Most rivers and lakes are freshwater. Oceans are saltwater.

The Water Cycle

2 The gas rises high into the sky where it forms clouds.

1 The Sun causes water to warm up and evaporate. This means water turns into a gas.

3 Over time, the clouds become too heavy for the air to hold. Water falls back to Earth as rain or snow. This is called precipitation.

4 The water that falls to Earth is collected in rivers, lakes, and oceans. The water cycle can then start over again.

How is Water Cleaned?

Pollutants are left behind when water evaporates during the water cycle. If there is too much pollution, water cannot be properly cleaned during evaporation.

Water is filtered before entering people's homes. Filters remove dirt and germs from water. This makes it safe for people to drink water.

Water Around the World

Brazil has the most freshwater of any country. Papua New Guinea, India, and Pakistan all have very little freshwater.

Lake Baikal in Russia is the largest and oldest freshwater lake in the world. The largest collection of ocean pollution is found in the Pacific ocean. One of the largest drinking water treatment plants is the Wylie Water Treatment Plant in Texas.

Arctic Ocean

Asia

Lake Baikal

North America

Pacific Ocean

Pacific Ocean

Texas

Australia

0   2,000 miles

0   4,000 kilometers

N

Legend
Land
Ocean

Why is Water Important?

All living things on Earth need water to survive. This includes animals, insects, and plants.

Water is needed to keep people and their environments clean. People can become sick if they do not have clean water to help wash germs away.

What is Water Pollution?

Water pollution is when waste or chemicals enter bodies of water like oceans, rivers, or lakes. **Pesticides**, garbage, and oil spills are all kinds of pollution.

KEY WORD

Pesticides: chemicals sprayed on fruits and vegetables to keep insects away.

Most water pollution comes from sewage or **industrial waste**. People have created so much water pollution that water can no longer be cleaned properly during the water cycle.

KEY WORD

Industrial waste: waste leftover from the creation of buildings or mines.

Water Pollution Facts

About 12 billion pounds (5.4 billion kilograms) of garbage ends up in oceans every year.

About forty percent of lakes in the United States are not safe for swimming.

About eighty percent of ocean pollution comes from land.

Over 1.2 trillion gallons (4.5 trillion liters) of sewage and industrial waste pollute water in the United States every year.

The United States uses about 2.2 billion pounds (998 million kg) of pesticides every year.

Water pollution has created about 500 areas around the world where no living thing can live or grow.

How Water Pollution Affects Animals

Chemicals in the water can make it hard for fish to breathe. Land animals can become very sick if they drink polluted water.

Many animals that live in the water confuse garbage with food. Eating garbage can make them sick.

How Water Pollution Affects Humans

Polluted water contains many viruses and diseases. This can make people very sick if they drink or swim in polluted water. About 1.8 million people died in 2015 from drinking polluted water.

Around 700 million people do not have access to clean water. In Africa, many people walk for about 3.7 miles (6 kilometers) to get clean water. This is the same as walking around a football field 15 times.

How Water Pollution Affects Earth

Many of the chemicals in polluted water kill plants. These chemicals can also destroy the nutrients in soil. This makes it hard for new plants to grow.

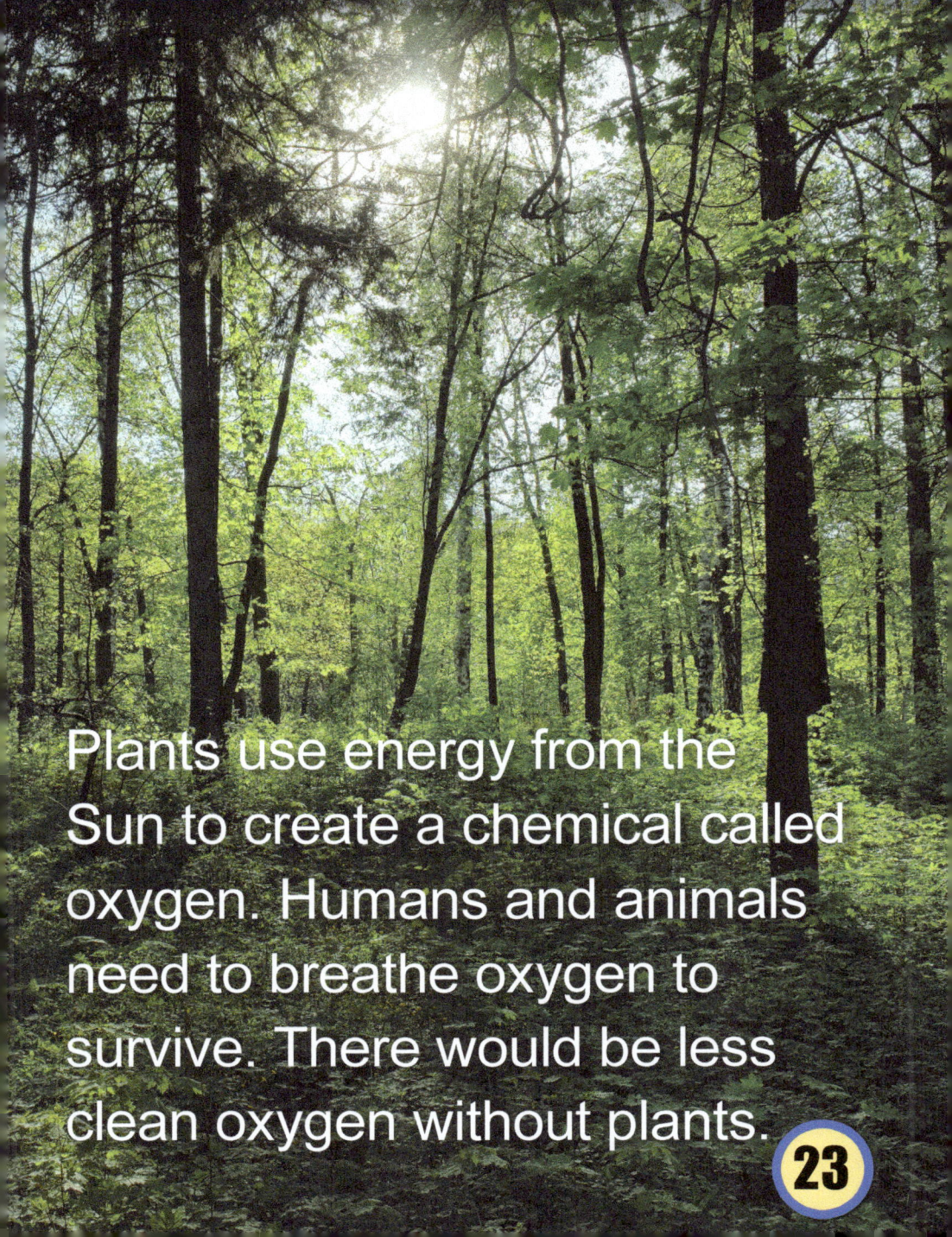

Plants use energy from the Sun to create a chemical called oxygen. Humans and animals need to breathe oxygen to survive. There would be less clean oxygen without plants.

Water Conservation

Water conservation means using less water and cutting back on water wasting habits. This helps to save Earth's clean water so there is enough for everyone.

Simple ways to conserve water at home include taking shorter showers and turning off the water while you brush your teeth.

Cleaning Up Water Pollution

Some companies are making small water filters that can be carried in your pocket. This helps people clean polluted water before use.

The Ocean Cleanup is cleaning garbage out of rivers. Boats collect plastic before it can reach the ocean. This helps keep animals that live in the ocean safe.

The Future of Water Conservation

The average American family wastes 180 gallons (681 liters) of water every week. This is the same amount of water it takes to do about 300 loads of laundry.

To help reduce water waste, many companies are creating products like taps and toilets that use less water.

Quiz

Test your knowledge of water by answering the following questions. The questions are based on what you have read in this book. The answers are listed on the bottom of the next page.

1 What percentage of Earth is covered in water?

2 What country has the most freshwater?

3 Where does most water pollution come from?

4 What can happen to land animals if they drink polluted water?

5 How many people do not have access to clean water?

6 What is water conservation?

Explore other level 2 readers.

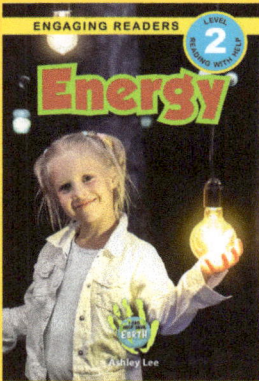

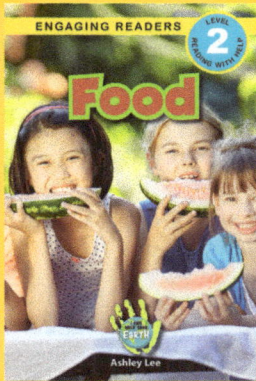

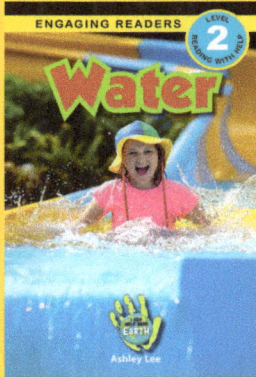

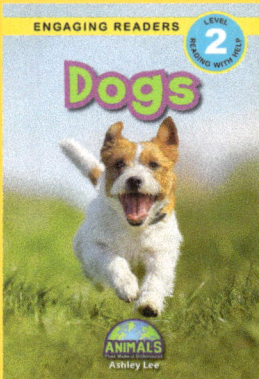

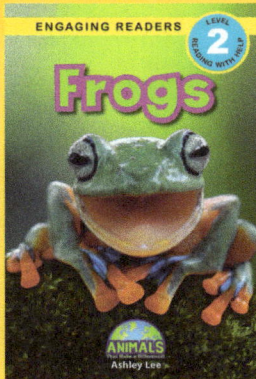

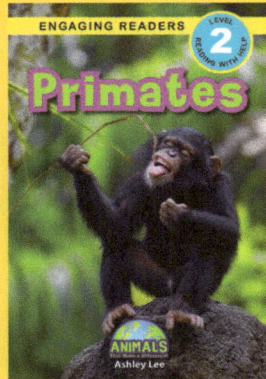

Visit www.engagebooks.com to explore more Engaging Readers.

Answers: 1. Almost seventy percent. 2. Brazil 3. Sewage and industrial waste. 4. They can become very sick. 5. Around 700 million 6. Using less water.

www.ingramcontent.com/pod-product-compliance
Lightning Source LLC
Chambersburg PA
CBHW051241020426
42331CB00016B/3474